Smile please! 1

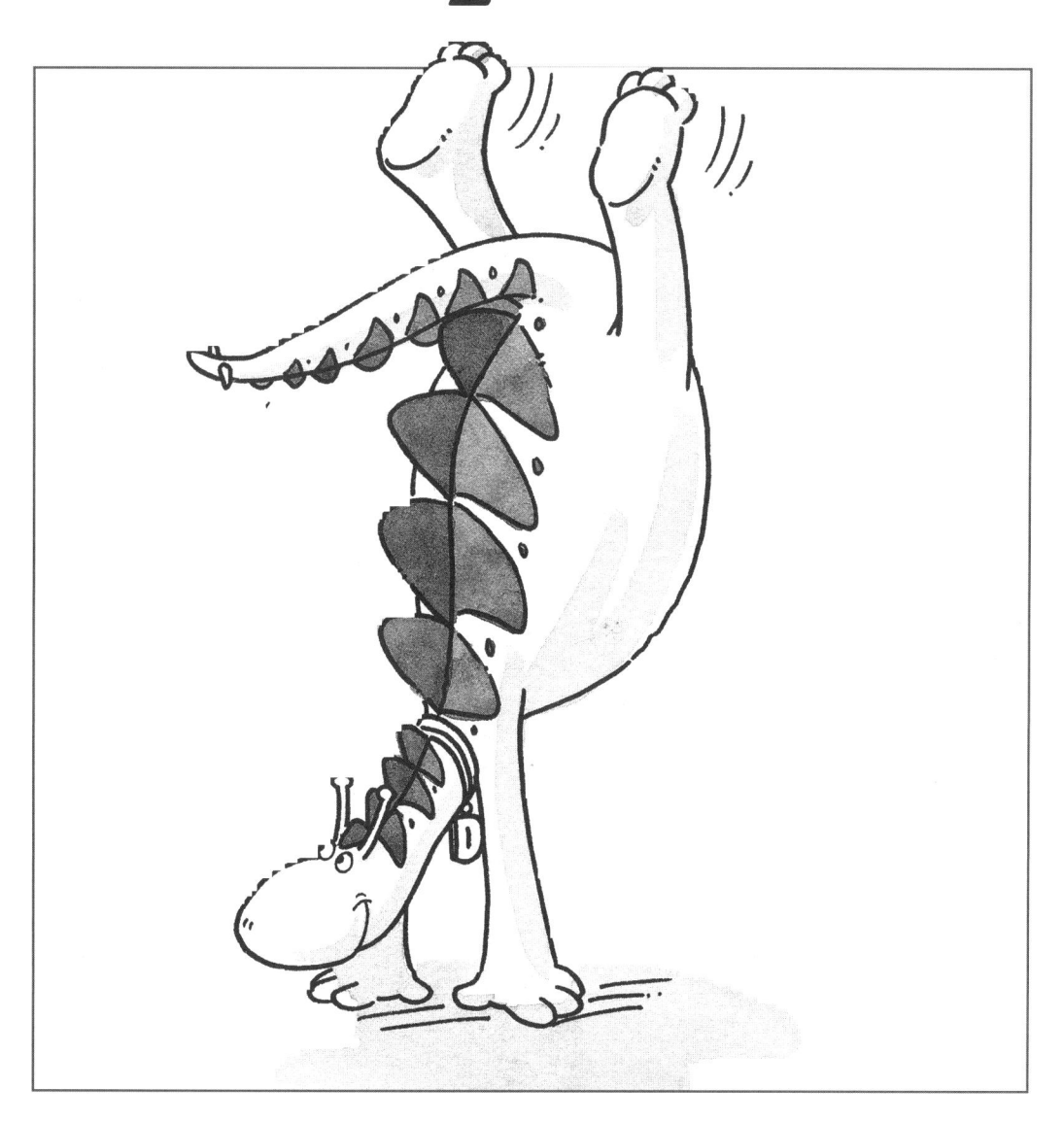

Workbook

Gabby Pritchard
Additional material by Jeanne Perrett-Tamami

Unit 1 Hello!

1. Trace the names.

2. Trace and colour.

Unit 1

3. Trace and match.

Sam

Maria

Toby

Kate

Ken

4. Draw yourself. Write.

I'm _____.

Unit 1

5. Find and join.

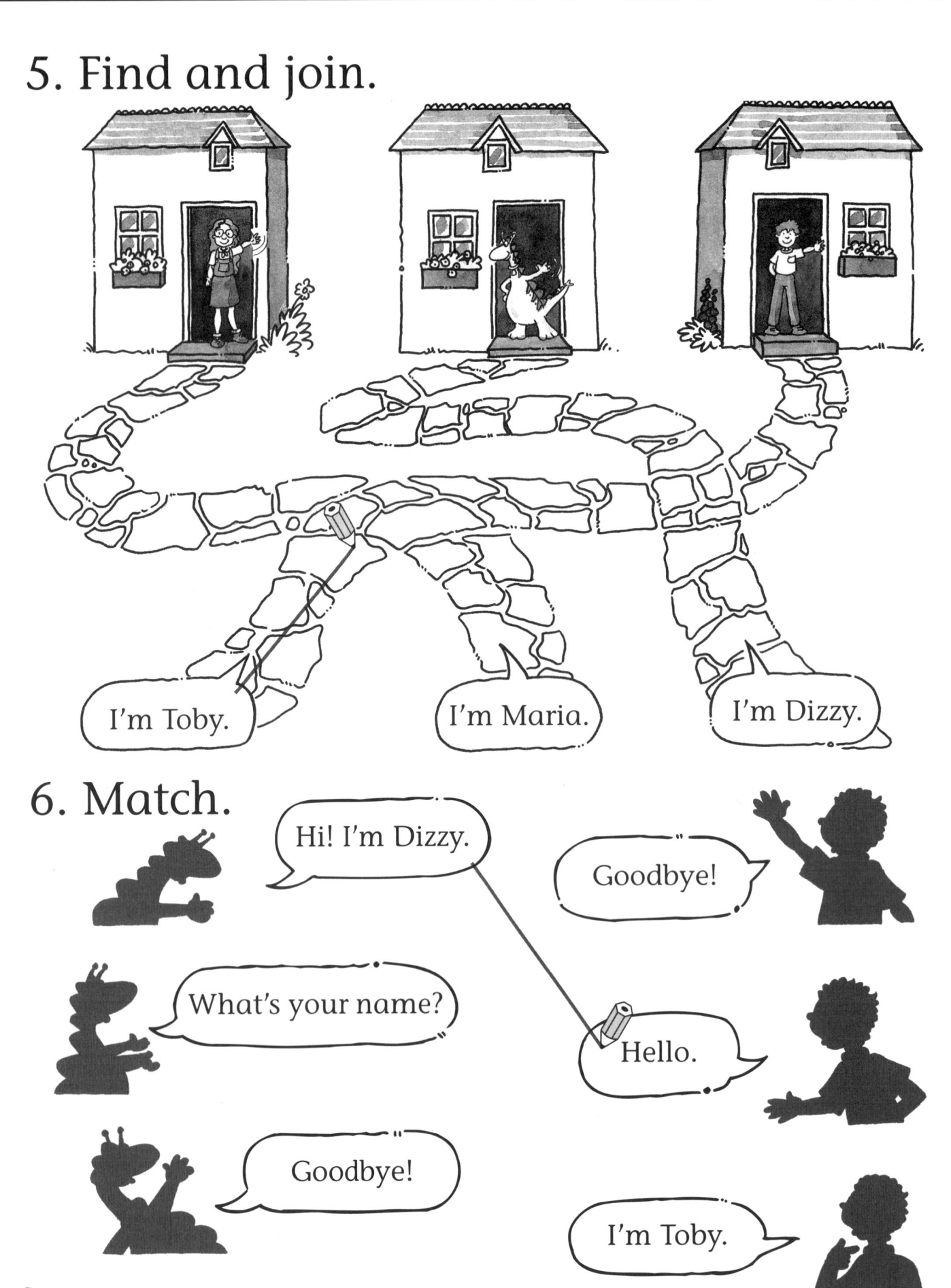

I'm Toby.   I'm Maria.   I'm Dizzy.

6. Match.

Hi! I'm Dizzy.

What's your name?

Goodbye!

Goodbye!

Hello.

I'm Toby.

Unit 1

7. Write.

Hi! I'm Maria.

I'm Toby.

__oodbye.

8. Write.

What's your name?

My name's Ken.

What's your name?

_____ Sam.

What's your name?

_____ Kate.

What's your name?

_____.

Unit 1

9. Match.

I'm Kate.   I'm Sam.   I'm Toby.   I'm Dizzy.

10. Circle the correct name.

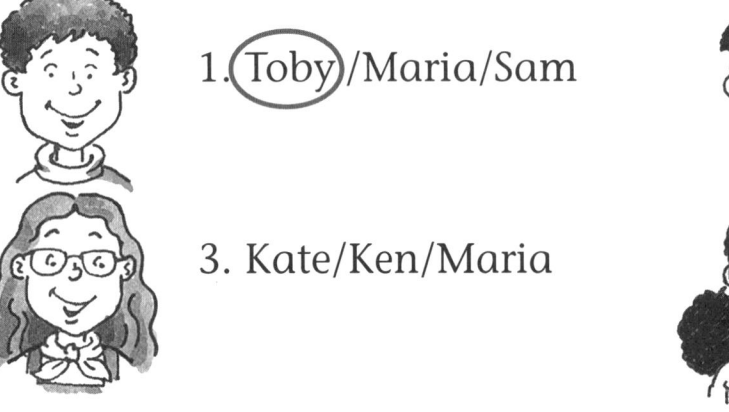

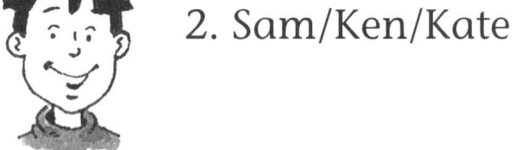

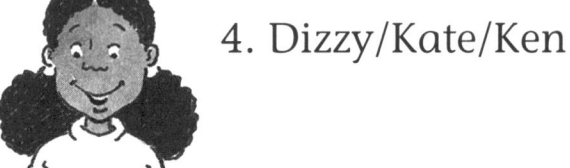

1. (Toby)/Maria/Sam

2. Sam/Ken/Kate

3. Kate/Ken/Maria

4. Dizzy/Kate/Ken

11. Write.

1. your/is/name?/What   What is your name?

2. name/is/Dizzy./My   _____

3. is/Toby./My/name   _____

4. am/Dizzy./I   _____

5. Toby./I/am   _____

Unit 1

6

12. Write I am/What is/My name is.

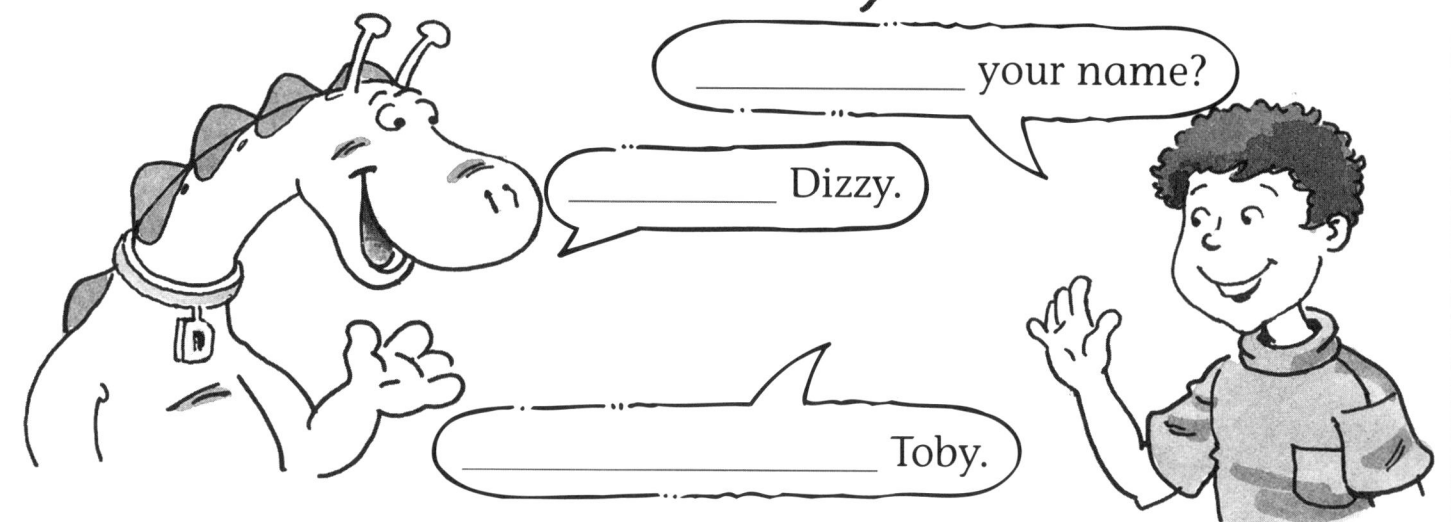

_____ your name?

_____ Dizzy.

_____ Toby.

13. Find and write.

ateK
1. Kate

izyDz
2. _____

neK
3. _____

aMiar
4. _____

amS
5. _____

obTy
6. _____

Unit 1

14. Write.   Goodbye!   I'm Toby.   ~~Hello!~~   I'm Sam.

1. Hello!

2. _____

3. _____

4. _____

Now I know

☐ Hello./Hi.
☐ What's your name?
☐ I'm …/My name is … .
☐ Goodbye.

Unit 1

Unit 2 Colours

1. Find, write and colour.

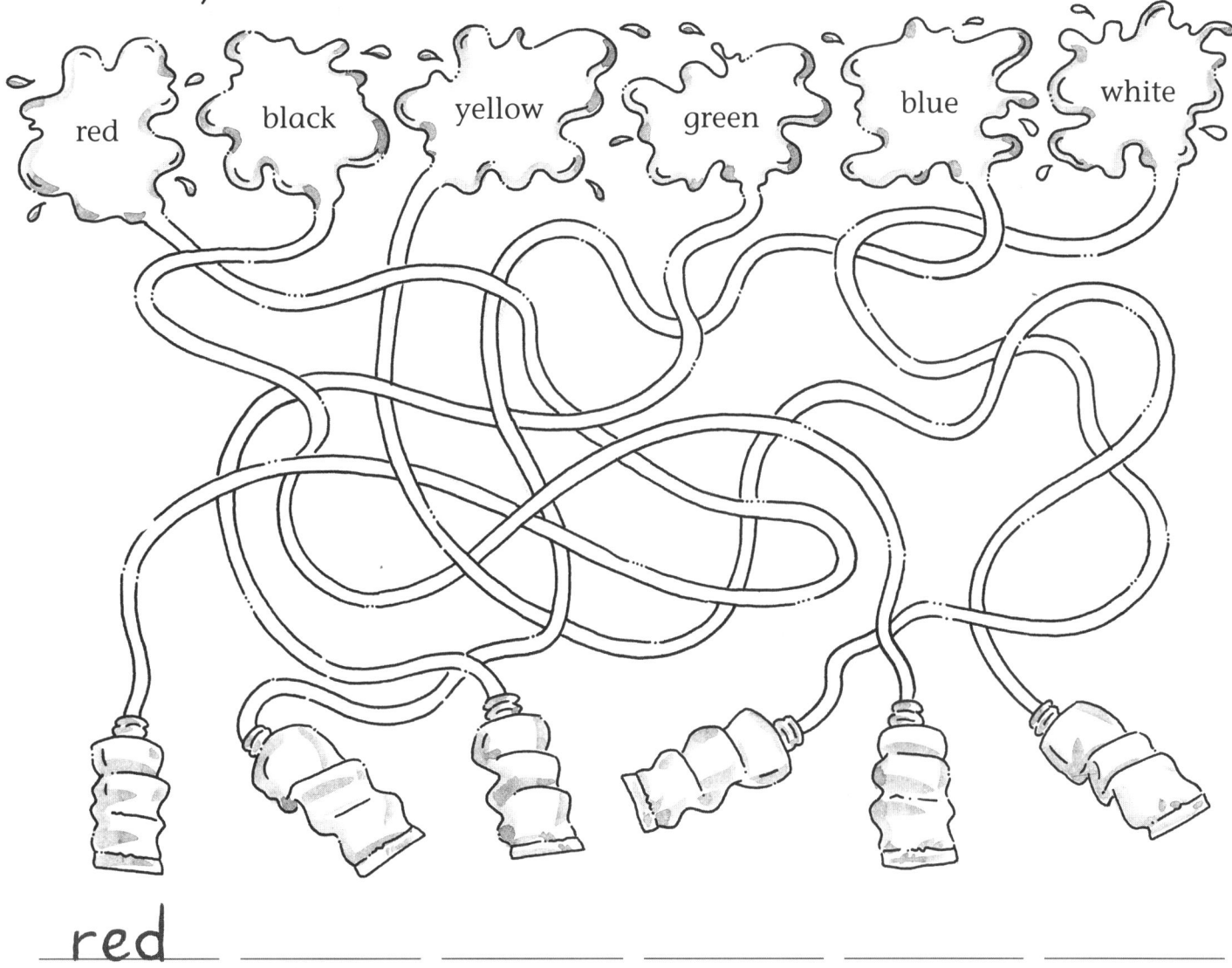

red   black   yellow   green   blue   white

red _____

2. Circle the colours.

(blue) redblackgreenyellowwhite

3. Trace and colour.

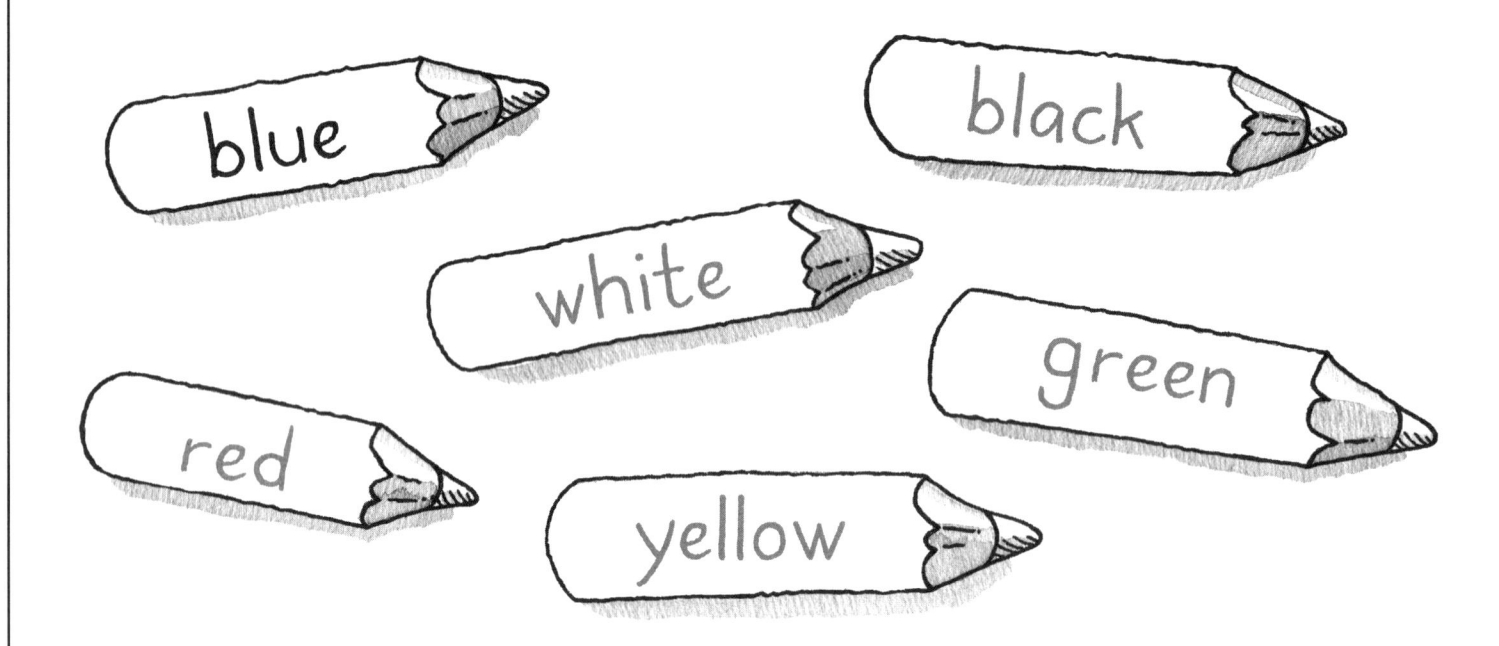

blue
black
white
green
red
yellow

4. Colour and write.

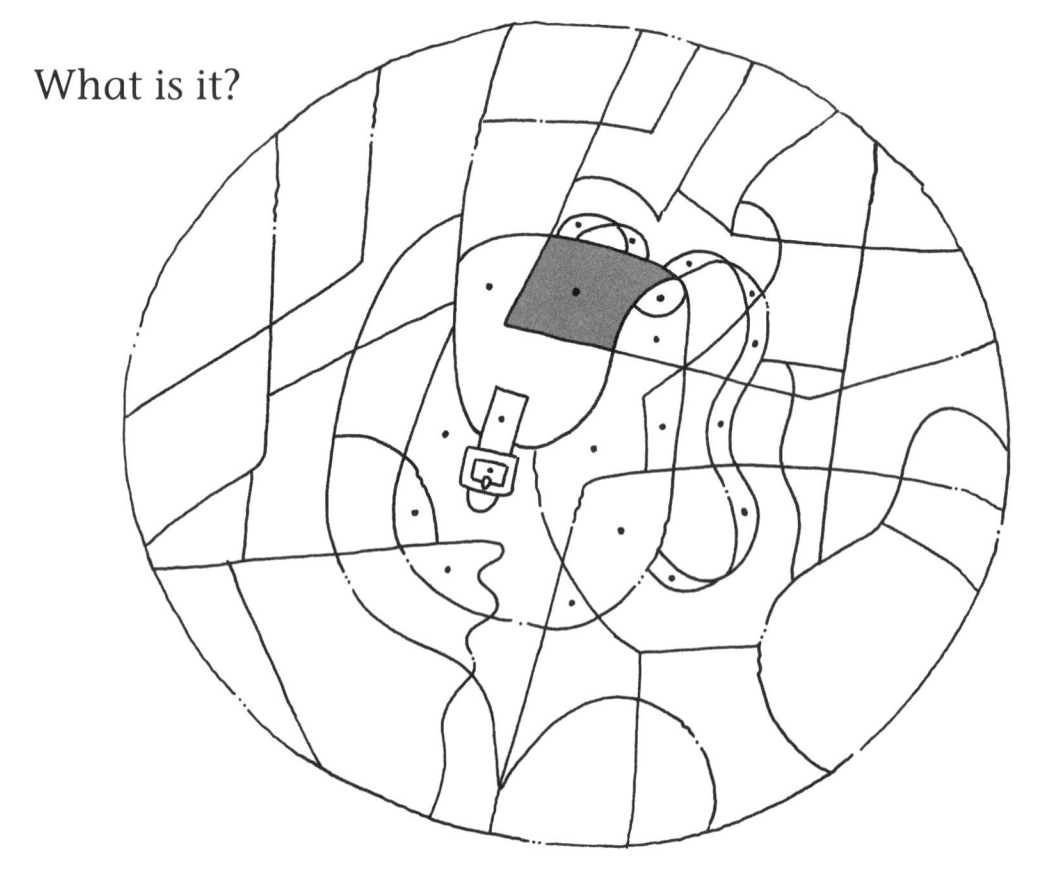

What is it?

It's a _____.

Unit 2

5. Join the dots. Write.

What is it?

It's a _____.

6. Find and circle.

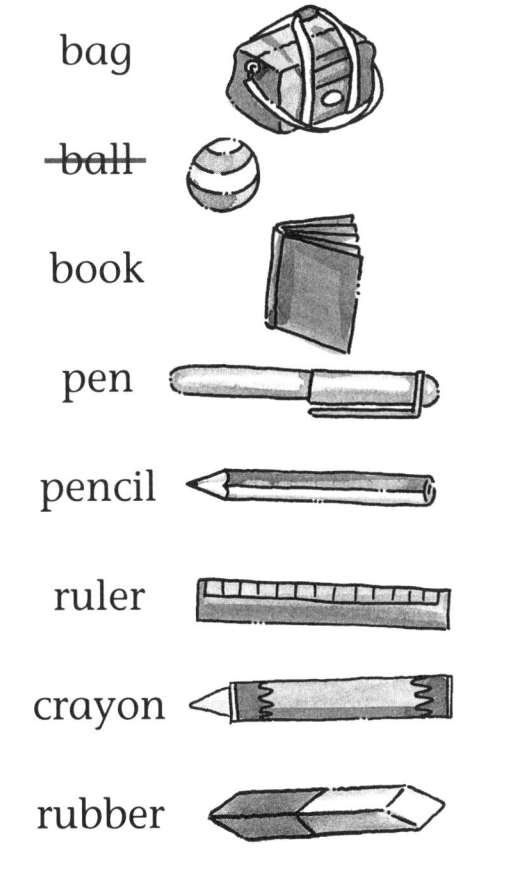

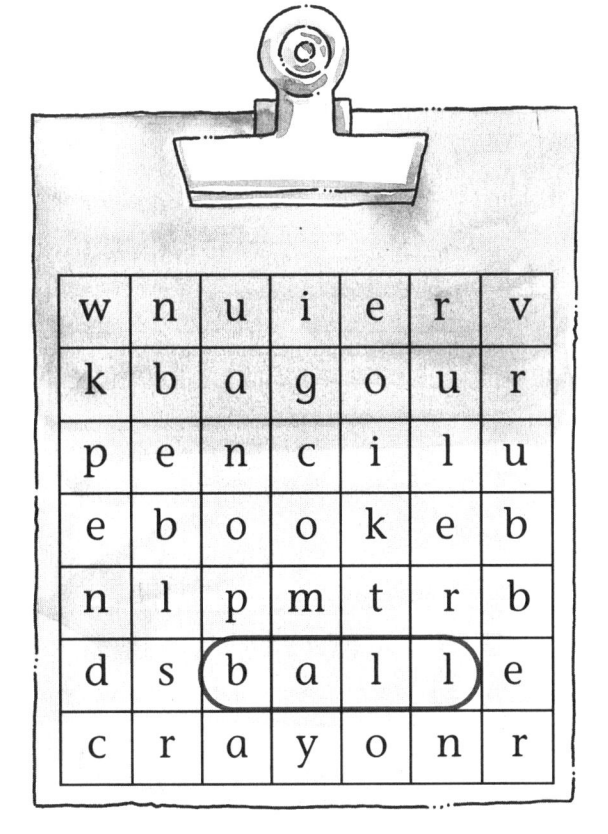

bag
~~ball~~
book
pen
pencil
ruler
crayon
rubber

w	n	u	i	e	r	v
k	b	a	g	o	u	r
p	e	n	c	i	l	u
e	b	o	o	k	e	b
n	l	p	m	t	r	b
d	s	b	a	l	l	e
c	r	a	y	o	n	r

Unit 2

7. Write and colour.

~~pen~~ pencil ruler bag book

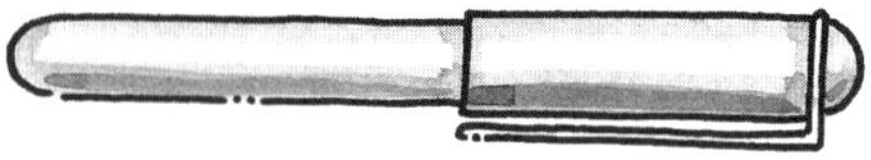

1. It's red. It's a **pen**.

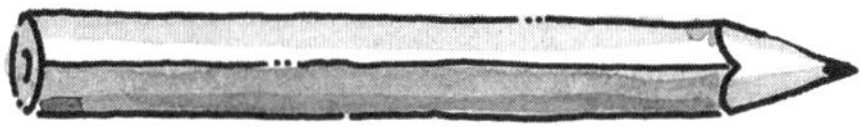

2. It's green. It's a _____.

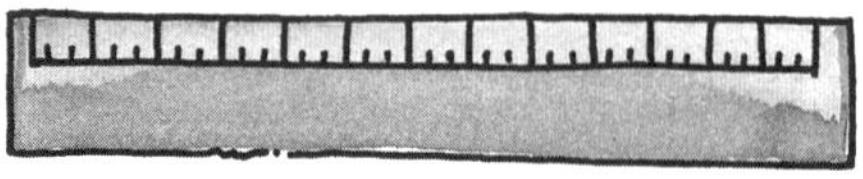

3. It's yellow. It's a _____.

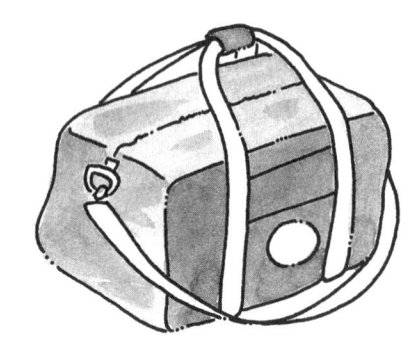

4. It's blue. It's a _____.

5. It's black. It's a _____.

8. Write.

1. What is it?
It's a **pencil**.

2. What is it?
It's a _____.

3. What is it?
It's _____.

4. What is _____?
_____.

5. What _____?
_____.

6. _____?
_____.

Unit 2

9. Read and colour.

1. It's a blue pencil.

2. It's a yellow rubber.

3. It's a red bag.

4. It's a green book.

5. It's a black pen.

6. It's a blue ruler.

10. Write It is and complete.

1. It's a cat.
   <u>It is a cat</u>.

2. It's a lion.
   _____.

3. It's a fish.
   _____.

4. It's a monkey.
   _____.

5. It's a rabbit.
   _____.

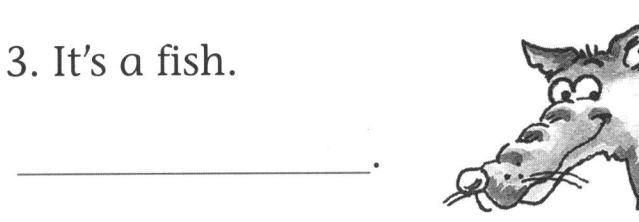

6. It's a wolf.
   _____.

Unit 2

11. Write and colour.

1. It's/red/bag./a
   It's a red bag.

2. wolf./a/It's/white
   _____

3. blue/pen./a/It's
   _____

4. a/It's/monkey./black
   _____

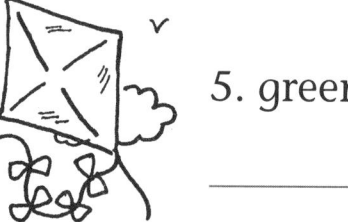

5. green/kite./a/It's
   _____

6. a/fish./yellow/It's
   _____

12. Write and colour.

1. It's black.
   What is it?
   It's a book.

2. It's red.
   What is _____?
   _____.

3. It's blue.
   What _____?
   _____.

4. It's green.
   _____?
   _____.

5. It's yellow.
   _____?
   _____.

6. ____ white.
   _____?
   _____.

Unit 2

13. Colour the robot.

- a red
- b green
- c black
- d blue
- e white
- f yellow

Now I know

- ☐ What is it?
- ☐ It's a … .
- ☐ It's blue.
- ☐ Colours

Unit 2

Unit 3   How old are you?

1. Say and write the numbers.

   1 2 3
   5   9
     7

2. Write and draw.

   H_____ B_____

   I'm _____

3. Write and colour.

H_____
_____ you?

I'm

4. Draw and answer for you.

I'm 10.

I'm _____.

5. Look and write.

How old are you?

I'm three.

I'm _____.

I'm _____.

I'm six

I'm eight

6. Trace and match.

one   five   six   nine

1 2 3 4 5 6 7 8 9 10

three   eight

two   four   seven   ten

7. Look and write.

What's number 1? It's a __computer game__.

What's number 2? It's a t_____ b_____.

What's number 3? It's a b_____.

What's number 4? It's a b_____.

What's number 5? It's a t_____.

What's number 6? It's a d_____.

What's number 7? It's a p_____.

What's number 8? It's a c_____.

What's number 9? It's a c_____.

What's number 10? It's a r_____.

Unit 3

8. Look and match.

1. He is six.   She's three.

2. She is three.   He's ten.

3. He is five.   She's four.

4. She is seven.   He's six.

5. She is four.   He's five.

6. He is ten.   She's seven.

9. Write.

1. <u>He's ten</u>.

2. _____.

3. _____.

4. _____.

5. _____.

6. _____.

Unit 3   20

10. Write.

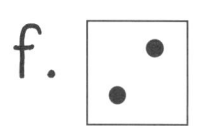

a.  [1] + [6] = <u>seven</u>　　d.  [3] + [5] = _____

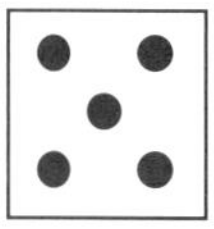

b. 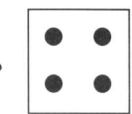 [4] + [2] = _____　　e. 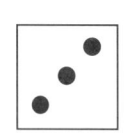 [3] + [2] = _____

c. 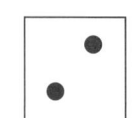 [2] + [6] = _____　　f. [3] + [1] = _____

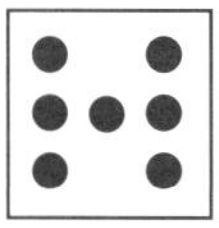

11. Look and write.

Thank you for the <u>book</u>.

Thank you for the _____.

Thank you for the _____.

12. Look and write his or her.

1. It's <u>his</u> bag.

2. It's _____ book.

3. It's _____ pencil.

4. It's _____ ruler.

5. It's _____ rubber.

6. It's _____ ball.

21　　Unit 3

13. Join the dots and write.

I'm s_____.

Now I know

- [ ] Happy Birthday!
- [ ] How old are you?
- [ ] I'm/He's/She's ... .
- [ ] Numbers 1 – 10
- [ ] Thank you for the ... .
- [ ] his/her

Unit 3

Unit 4 — Is it a plane?

1. Write.

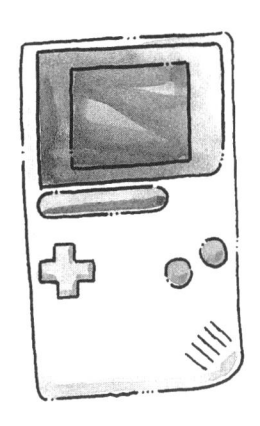

1. c _____

2. _____

3. _____

2. Complete with ✗ or ✓.

Is it a train?	Is it a kite?	Is it a doll?	Is it a plane?	Is it a car?
1. ✓	2. ☐	3. ☐	4. ☐	5. ☐

3. Write Yes or No.

Is it a bike?   Is it a boat?    Is it a doll?

1. __No__, it isn't.   2. _____, it isn't.   3. _____, it is.

4. Write.

__Is it__ a plane?

No, _____.

_____ a car?

Yes, _____.

Unit 4

5. Find and circle.

1. kite / (boat) / bike / doll
2. boat / kite / bike / doll
3. bike / plane / car / kite
4. car / bike / boat / plane

6. Write.

```
        1
      2   o   3
              r       6p   7c
    4     l
         5d  i  n  o  s  a  u  r
                   8     i
```

25

Unit 4

7. Write Yes, it is or No, it isn't.

1. Is it a ball?

   Yes, it is.

2. Is it a plane?

   _____.

3. Is it a rabbit?

   _____.

4. Is it a robot?

   _____.

5. Is it a dinosaur?

   _____.

8. Write.

1. It's a bike.
2. _____.
3. _____. 
4. _____.
5. _____.
6. _____.

9. Look and write.

It begins with B.

_____ it a boat?

No, it _____.

_____ a bike?

Yes, it _____.

27　　　　Unit 4

10. Write.

1. it/Is/a/bike?
   <u>Is it a bike?</u>

2. a/boat?/it/Is
   _____

3. it/a/Is/kite?
   _____

4. Is/train?/a/it
   _____

11. Write the questions.

1. <u>Is it a bike?</u> 
Yes, it is.

2. _____
No, it isn't.

3. _____ 
Yes, it is.

4. _____ 
No, it isn't.

5. _____ 
No, it isn't.

6. _____ 
Yes, it is.

Unit 4   28

12. Find and circle.

s	b	u	t	k	d	f
m	a	b	b	i	k	e
z	l	o	v	t	o	t
p	l	a	n	e	l	r
y	o	t	r	i	n	a
b	a	d	o	l	l	i
k	i	m	c	a	r	n

ball
bike
boat
car
doll
kite
~~plane~~
train

Now I know

☐ Is it a … ?
☐ Yes, it is./No, it isn't.
☐ It begins with … .

Unit 4

Unit 5 Shapes

1. Count and write.

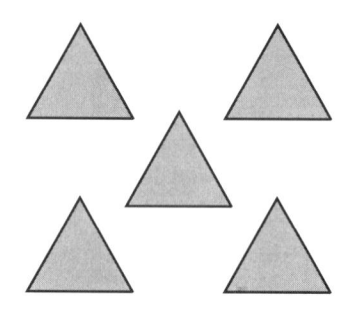

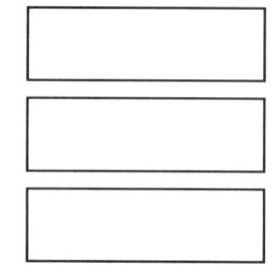

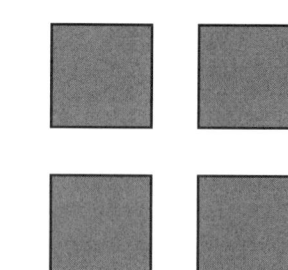

   <u> five </u>   _____   _____   _____
   triangles   rectangles   circles   squares

2. Count, write and colour.

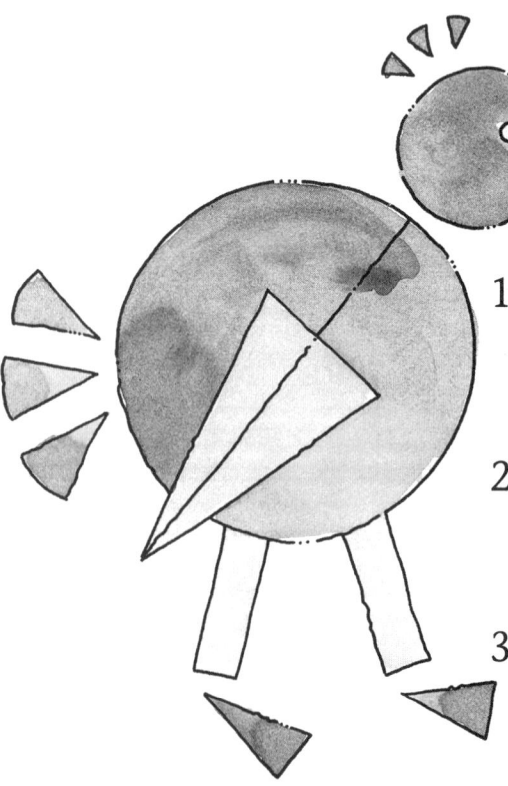

   1. How many circles are there?
      <u> three </u>

   2. How many triangles are there?
      _____

   3. How many rectangles are there?
      _____

Unit 5   30

3. Draw and say.

a square | a circle

a rectangle | a triangle

4. Colour and write.

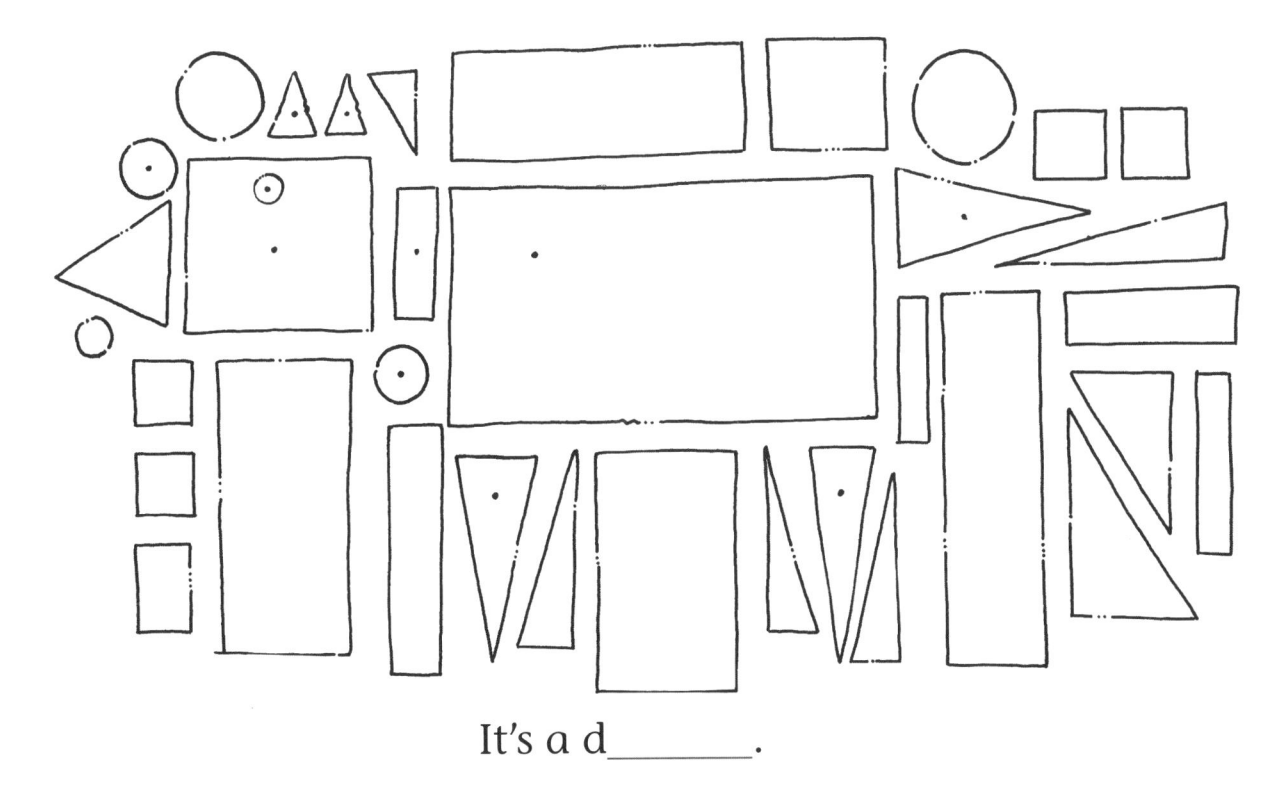

It's a d_____.

Unit 5

5. Write.

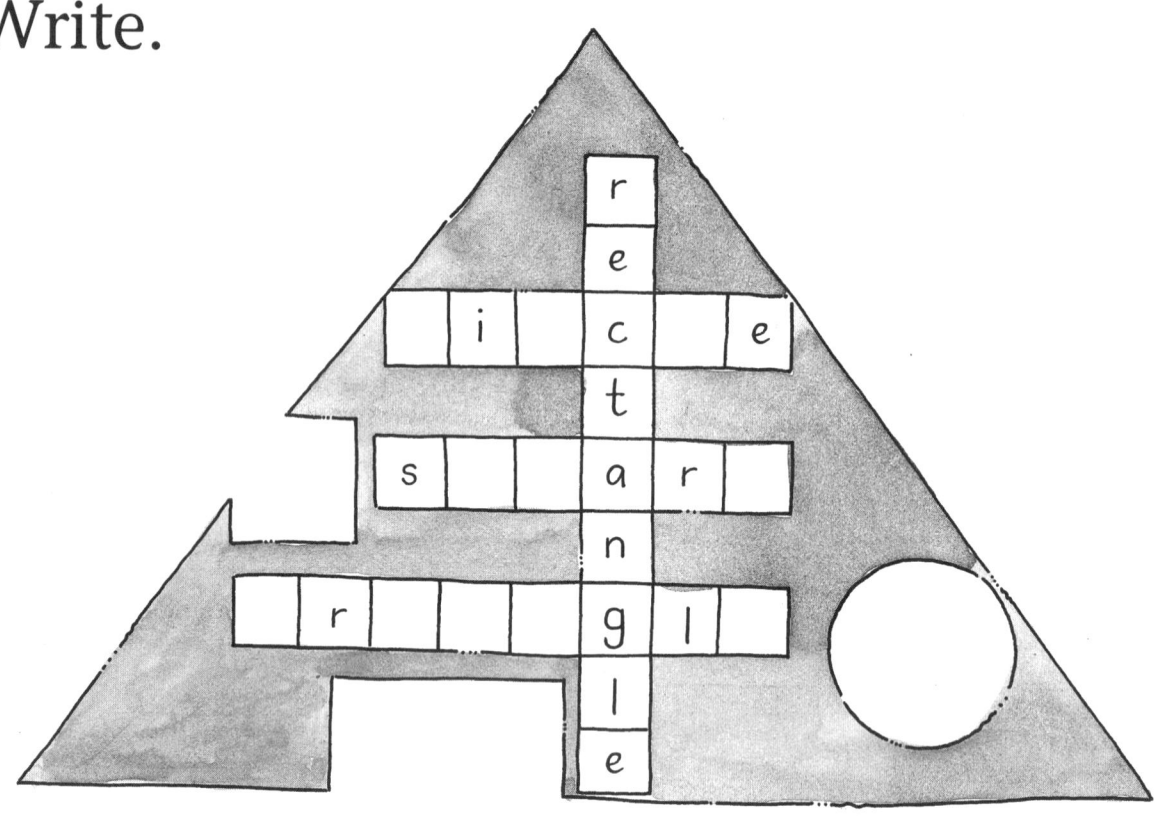

（crossword with letters: r, e, c, i, c, e, t, s, a, r, n, r, g, l, l, e — spelling rectangle, circle, square, triangle)

6. Write.

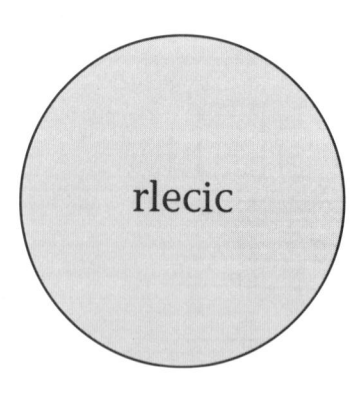

rlecic — 1. circle

nectrleag — 2. _____

usqrae — 3. _____

eilrtnag — 4. _____

Unit 5

7. Count and write.

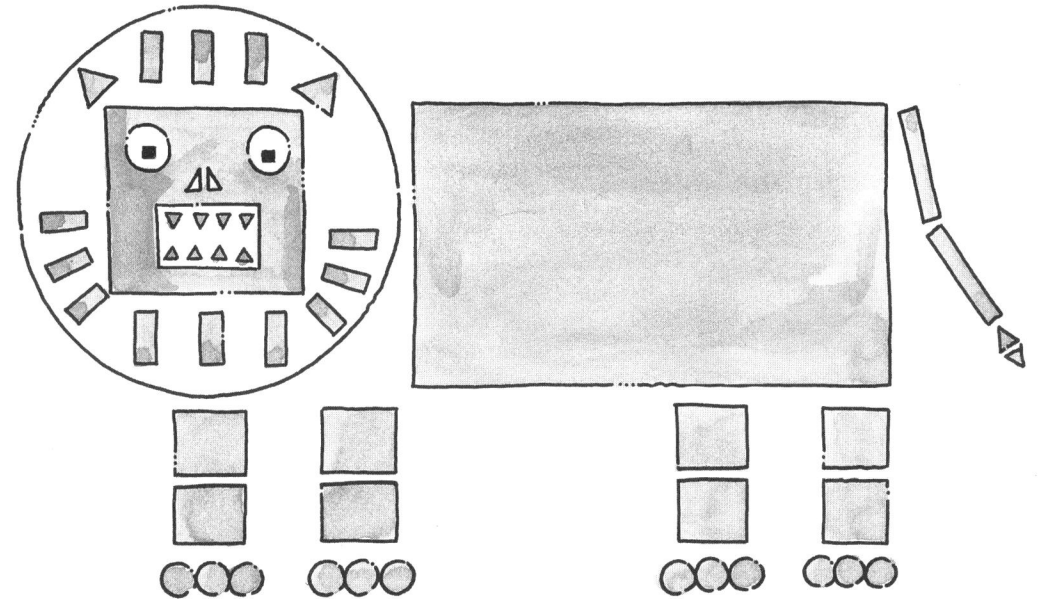

Is it a dog?

Is it a lion?

No, _____.

Yes, _____.

How many … are there?

1. There are __15__ circles.

2. There are ____ squares.

3. There are ____ triangles.

4. There are ____ rectangles.

33 Unit 5

8. Write.

a. [6 dots] + [5 dots] = <u>eleven</u>   d. [6 dots] + [6 dots] = _____

b. [6 dots] + [6 dots] = _____   e. [9 dots] + [6 dots] = _____

c. [9 dots] + [5 dots] = _____   f. [9 dots] + [9 dots] = _____

9. Write.

| 10+1 | 10+3 | 10+5 |

= <u>eleven</u>   = _____   = _____

| 10+6 | 10+8 | 10+10 |

= _____   = _____   = _____

Unit 5   34

10. Write There is or There are and complete.

1. <u>There are two cats</u>.

2. _____.

3. _____.

4. _____.

5. _____.

6. _____.

11. Write the numbers in the correct order.

14 16 11 18 20 17 12 19 15 13

a. <u>11 eleven</u>   b. _____   c. _____

d. _____   e. _____   f. _____

g. _____   h. _____   i. _____

j. _____

12. Use the shapes to draw the cat.
    Count and write.

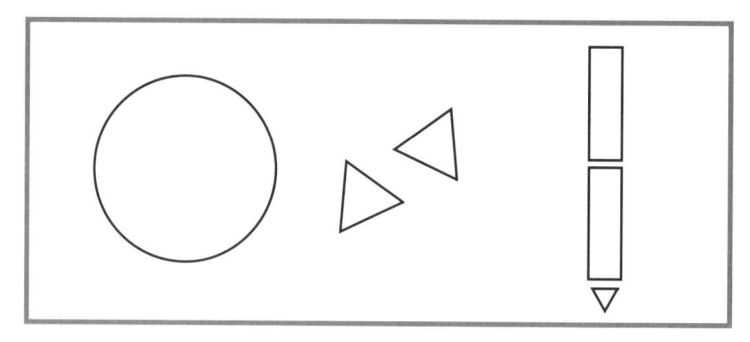

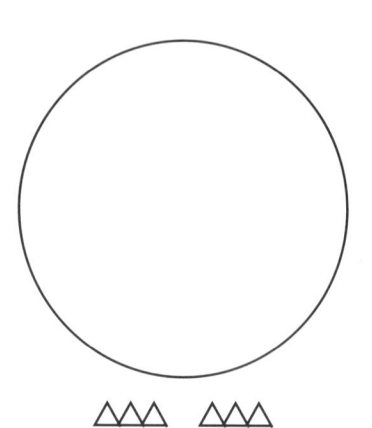

There are 9 triangles   .

There are _____ .

There are _____ .

Now I know

- [ ] How many ... are there?
- [ ] There is/There are ... .
- [ ] Numbers 11 – 20
- [ ] Shapes ○ △ □ ▭

Unit 5

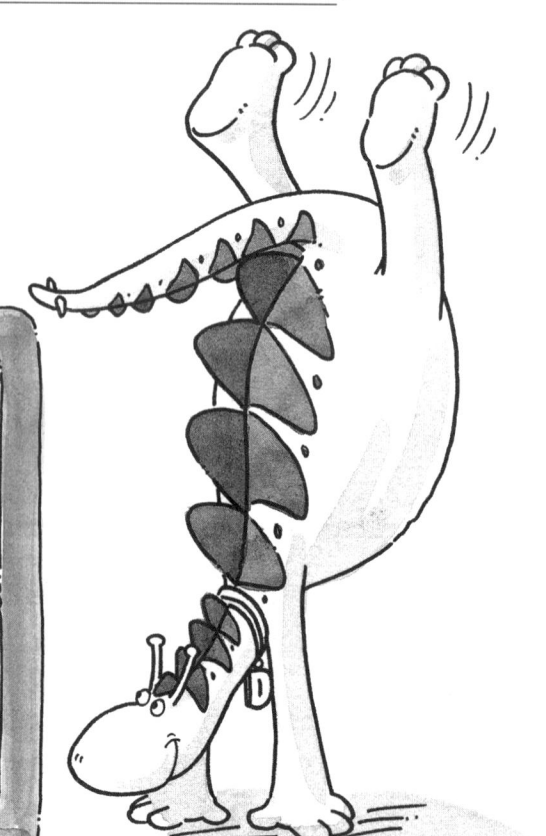

Unit 6   I'm reading.

1. Look and write.

I'm <u>listen</u>ing.

I'm _____ing.

I'm _____ing.

I'm _____ing.

2. Write.

What are you doing?

I'm learning E_____.

3. Write.

"I'm reading."

_____.

_____.

_____.

4. Write ✓ Yes or ✗ No.

1. What are you doing, Maria?
   I'm reading. ☐

2. What are you doing, Toby?
   I'm writing. ☐

3. What are you doing, Dizzy?
   I'm drawing. ☐

Unit 6   38

5. Write He or She.

1. Toby is sleeping.
   He is sleeping.

2. Maria is listening.
   _____ is listening.

3. Sam is writing.
   _____ is writing.

4. Ken is drawing.
   _____ is drawing.

6. Write He's or She's and complete.

1. He's reading.

2. _____.

3. _____.

4. _____.

5. _____.

6. _____.

7. Find and circle.

l	i	s	t	e	n	i	n	g	f
d	r	i	n	k	i	n	g	i	v
h	o	s	i	n	g	i	n	g	s
i	r	l	e	a	r	n	i	n	g
n	p	e	a	t	i	n	g	t	s
n	r	e	a	d	i	n	g	k	a
c	w	p	l	a	y	i	n	g	z
p	a	i	n	t	i	n	g	q	l
j	h	n	t	a	l	k	i	n	g
g	u	g	w	r	i	t	i	n	g

eating
~~drinking~~
learning
listening
painting
playing
reading
singing
sleeping
talking
writing

8. Write Yes, I am or No, I'm not.

1. Are you reading? Yes, I am.

2. Are you singing? _____.

3. Are you writing? _____.

4. Are you eating? _____.

Unit 6   40

9. Write.

1. He's talking. 2. _____. 3. _____.

4. _____. 5. _____. 6. _____.

Unit 6

10. Write.

1. he/What's/doing?
   What's he doing?

2. doing?/What's/she
   _____

3. he/doing?/What's
   _____

4. What's/doing?/Maria
   _____

5. Toby/doing?/What's
   _____

6. Dizzy/What's/doing?
   _____

11. Look and write.

~~eating~~   singing   sleeping   drinking

1. I'm _eating_. 
2. He's _____.
3. She's _____. 
4. She's _____.

Unit 6

12. Match.

1. He's drawing   a story.

2. She's writing   a song.

3. I'm singing   English.

4. She's learning   a picture.

5. He's reading   a hamburger.

6. She's eating   a book.

Now I know

- [ ] What are you doing?
- [ ] I'm ... .
- [ ] What's he/she doing?
- [ ] He's/She's ... .
- [ ] Are you ...ing?
- [ ] Yes, I am./No, I'm not.

Unit 7 Animals

1. Find and write.

1. 2.  3.  4.  5.

[2] ostrich   [ ] tiger   [ ] monkey   [ ] elephant   [ ] dinosaur

2. Look and write.

What's that?

1. It's an _elephant_.

2. It's an _____.

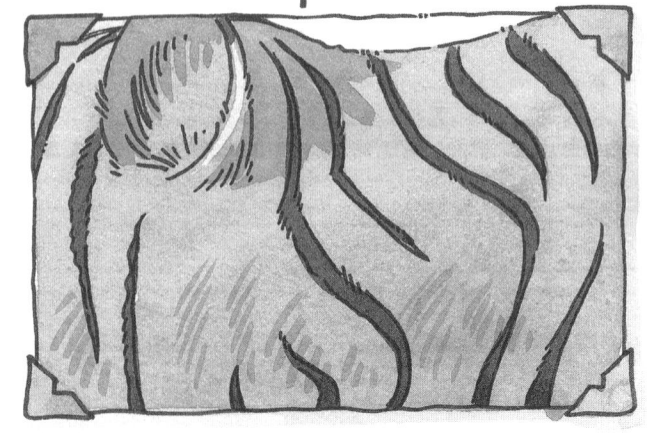

3. It's a _____.

4. It's a _____.

Unit 7   44

3. Look and write.

1. <u>elephant</u>

2. _____

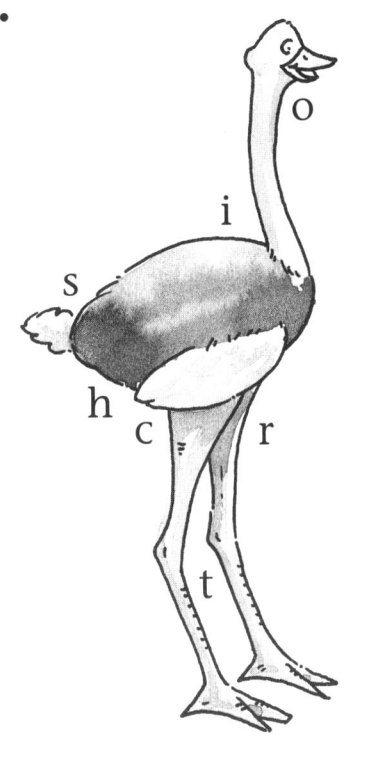

3. _____

4. _____

5. _____

4. Write.

1. <u>What's that</u>? <u>It's</u> a tiger.

2. _____? _____ an elephant.

3. _____? _____ an ostrich.

4. _____? _____ a monkey.

5. _____? _____ a dinosaur.

45   Unit 7

5. Find and circle.

m	o	n	k	e	y	v	c
o	s	t	r	i	c	h	y
u	f	r	t	i	g	e	r
s	a	w	z	e	b	r	a
e	l	e	p	h	a	n	t
s	n	a	k	e	m	i	d
g	i	r	a	f	f	e	k

elephant
giraffe
monkey
mouse
~~ostrich~~
snake
tiger
zebra

6. Write.

1. It's **big**.
It's a **bear**.

2. It's s_____.
It's a m_____.

3. It's l_____.
It's a s_____.

4. It's t_____.
It's a g_____.

Unit 7

7. Write a or an.

1. _a_ mouse   2. ___ elephant   3. ___ snake   4. ___ giraffe

5. ___ bear   6. ___ zebra   7. ___ ostrich

8. Read and draw.

It's long. It's green. It's a snake.

9. Write *is* or *are*.

1. This is an elephant.

2. These _____ bears.

3. These _____ snakes.

4. This _____ a monkey.

5. These _____ tigers.

6. This _____ a zebra.

Unit 7

10. Write This is or These are.

1. <u>These are</u> giraffes.

2. _____ a mouse.

3. _____ an ostrich.

4. _____ snakes.

11. Write That is or Those are.

1. <u>That is</u> a bear.

2. _____ a monkey.

3. _____ snakes.

4. _____ zebras.

Unit 7

12. Join the dots. Write.

What's that?

It's a _____.

Now I know

- [ ] What's that?
- [ ] It's a/an ... .
- [ ] It's big/small/tall/long/black.
- [ ] Yes it is./No it isn't.
- [ ] This/That is ... .
- [ ] These/Those are ... .

Unit 7

Christmas

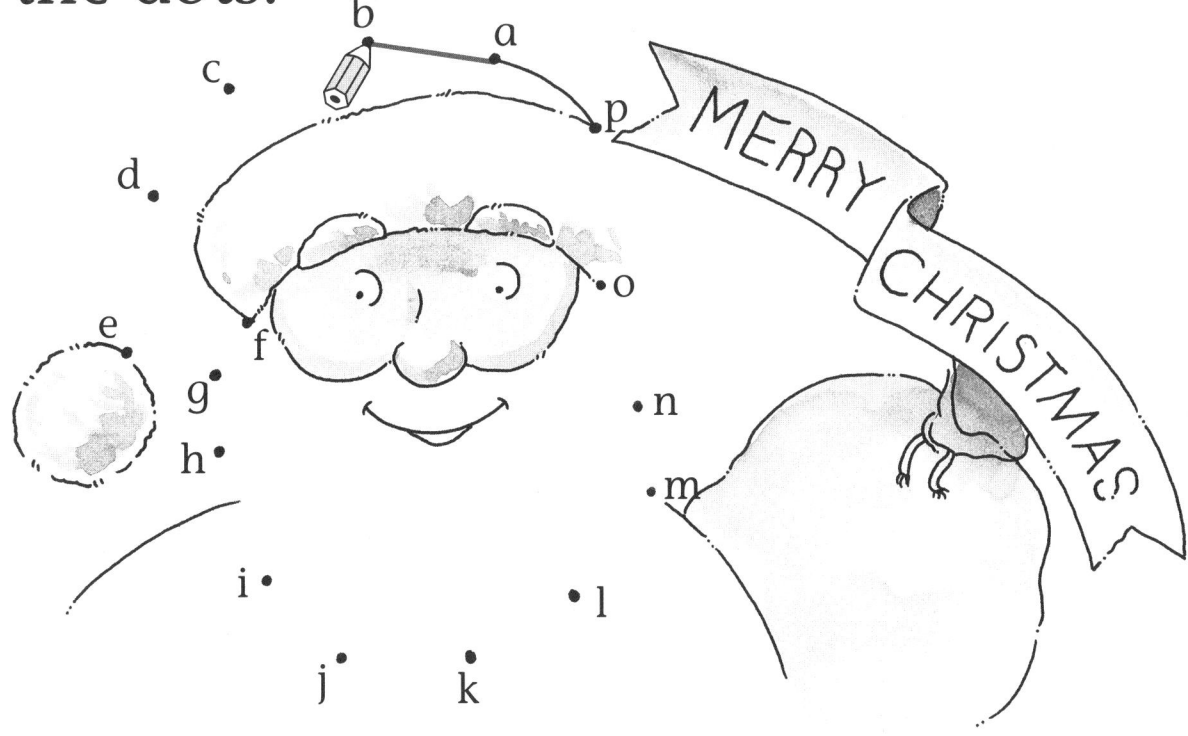

1. Trace and match.

doll   teddy bear   plane   train   ball

2. Join the dots.

MERRY CHRISTMAS

3. Match and colour.

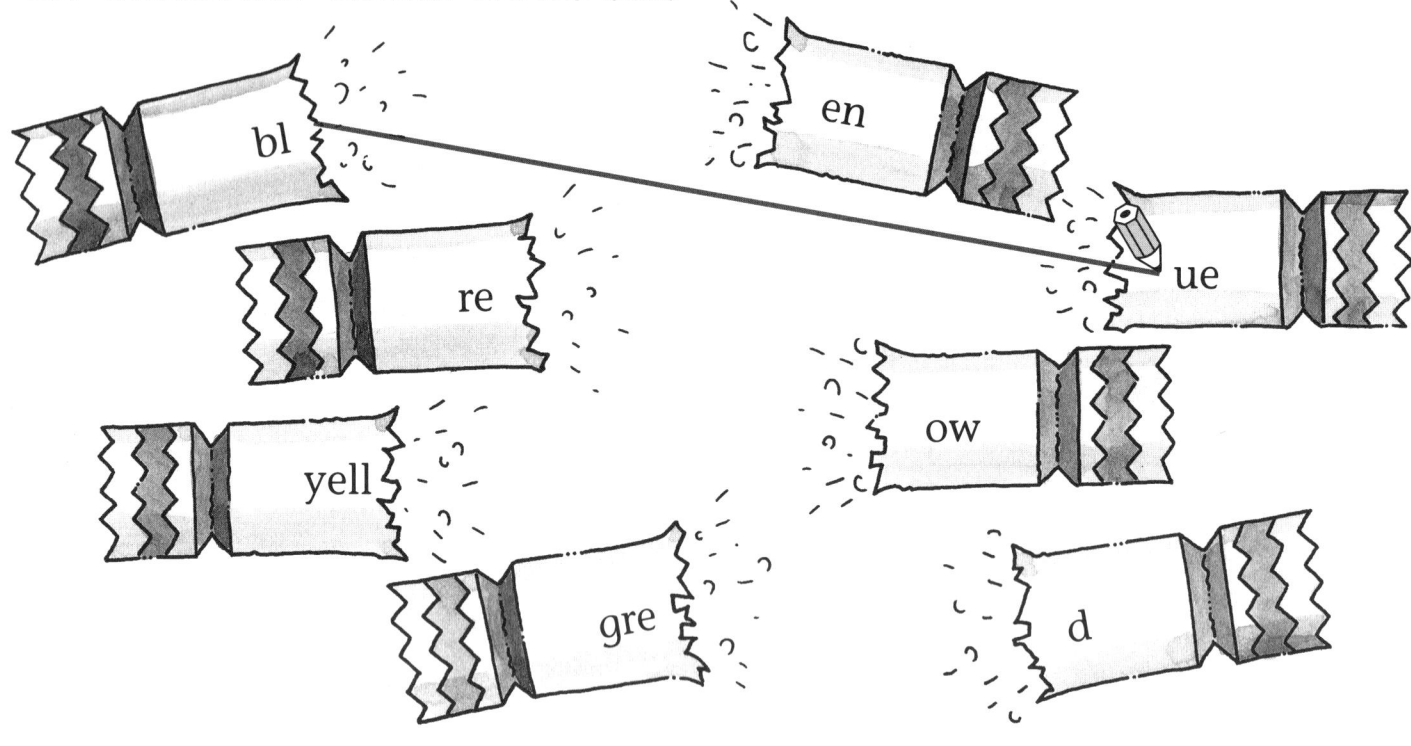

bl — en — ue — re — ow — yell — gre — d

4. Find the Christmas tree.

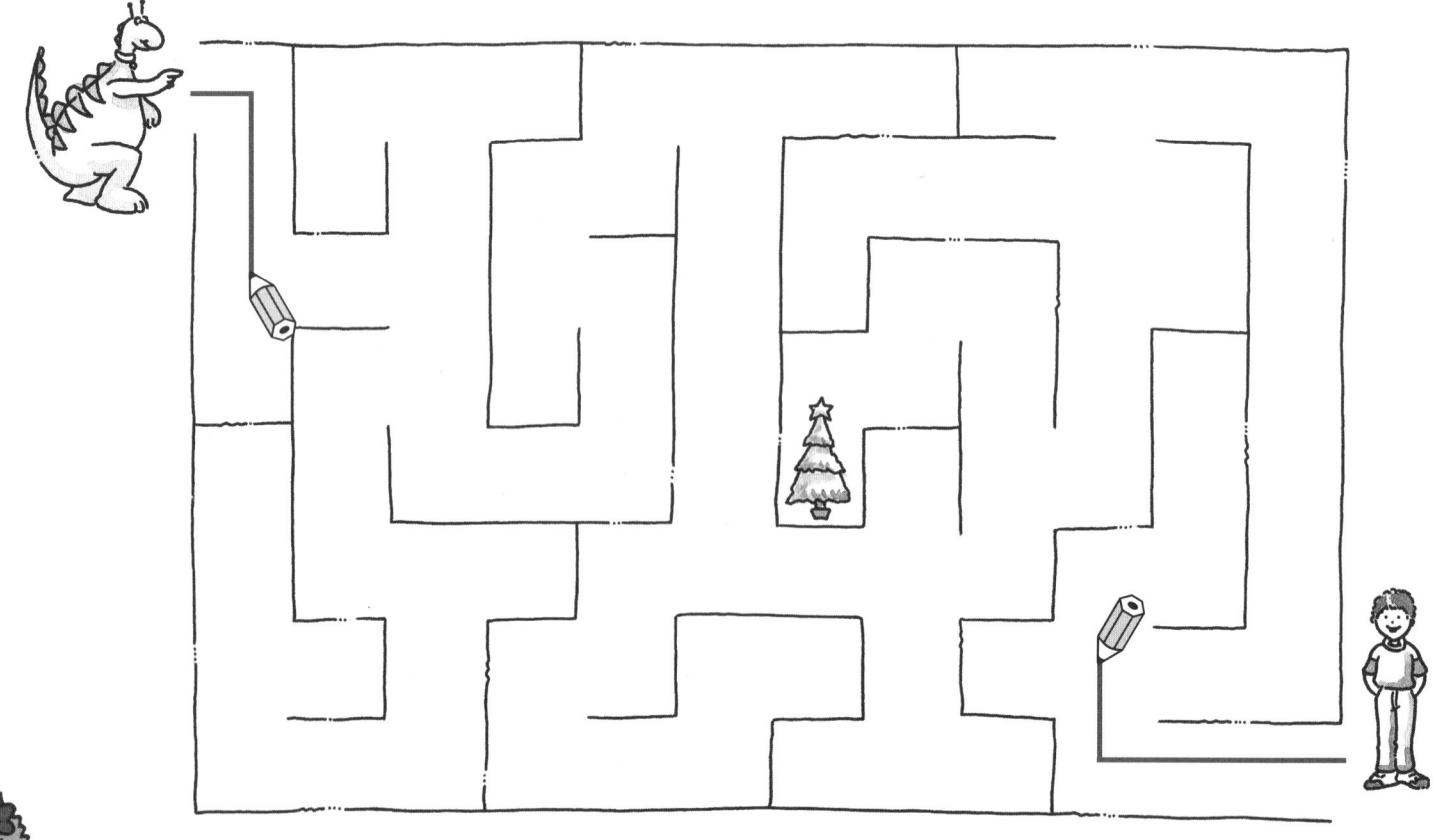

Christmas 52

5. Copy or trace and colour.

Christmas tree

star

reindeer

candle

bell

present

Christmas

Picture Dictionary

Cut out the pictures on pages 57 and 59. Stick them in the right place here to make your picture dictionary.

bag

teddy bear

dinosaur

doll

computer game

book

plane

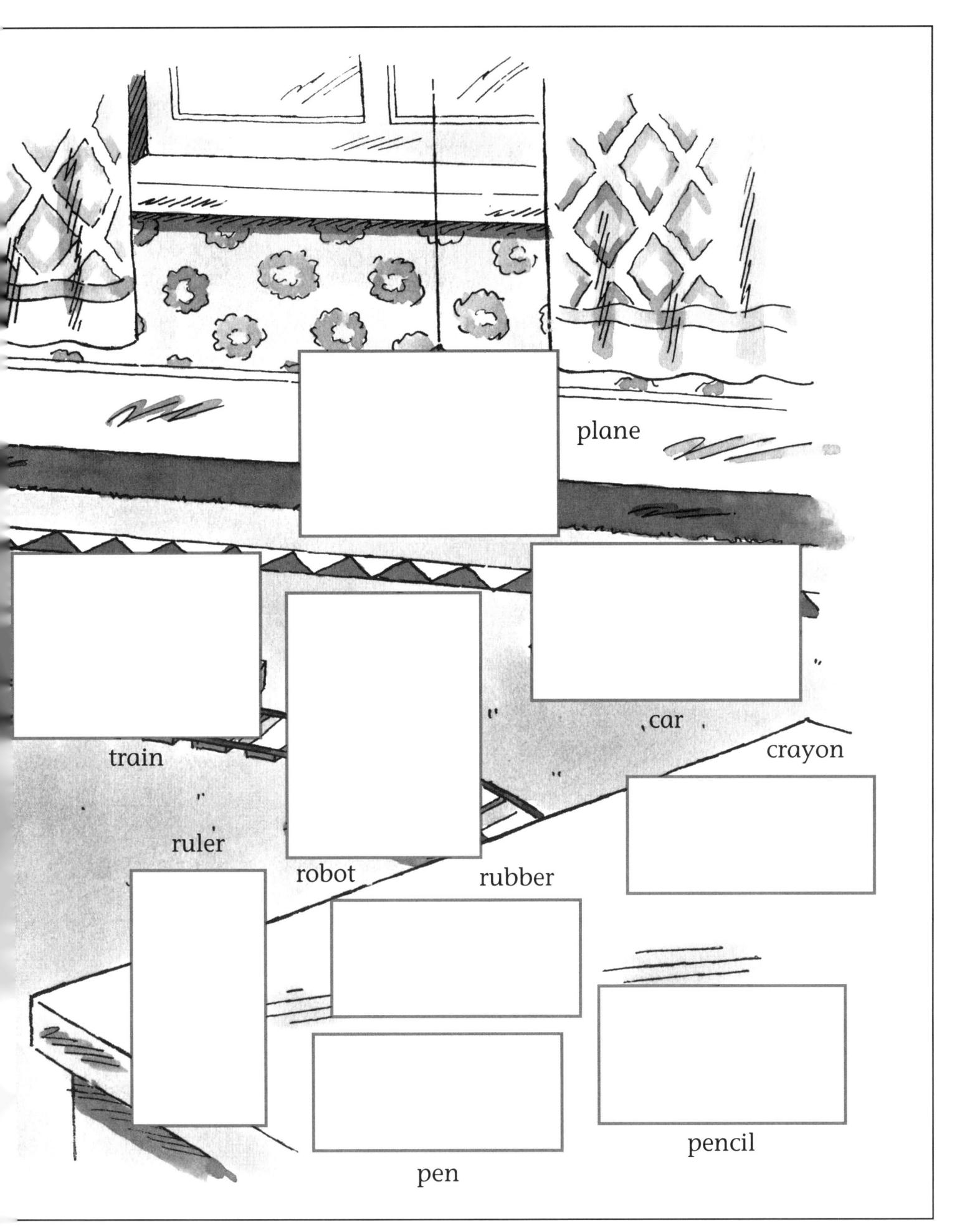

train

car

crayon

ruler

robot

rubber

pen

pencil

Cut out the words on page 61 and stick them in the right place here to make your picture dictionary.

Cut out these pictures and stick them in the right place on pages 54 and 55.

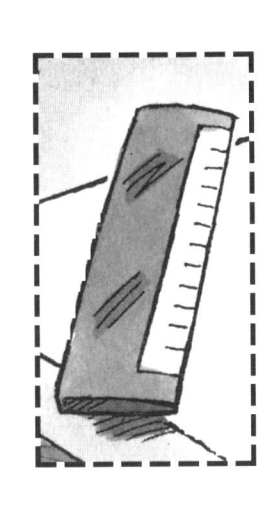

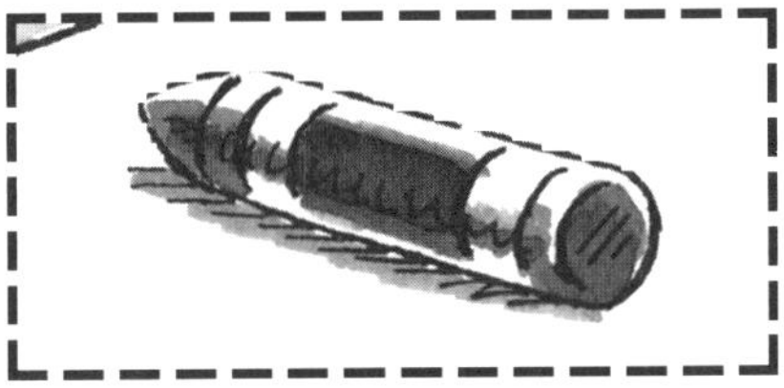

Cut out these pictures and stick them in the right place on pages 54 and 55.

Cut out these words and stick them in the right place on page 56.

ostrich	snake
tiger	bear
elephant	crocodile
giraffe	bird
mouse	frog

My year

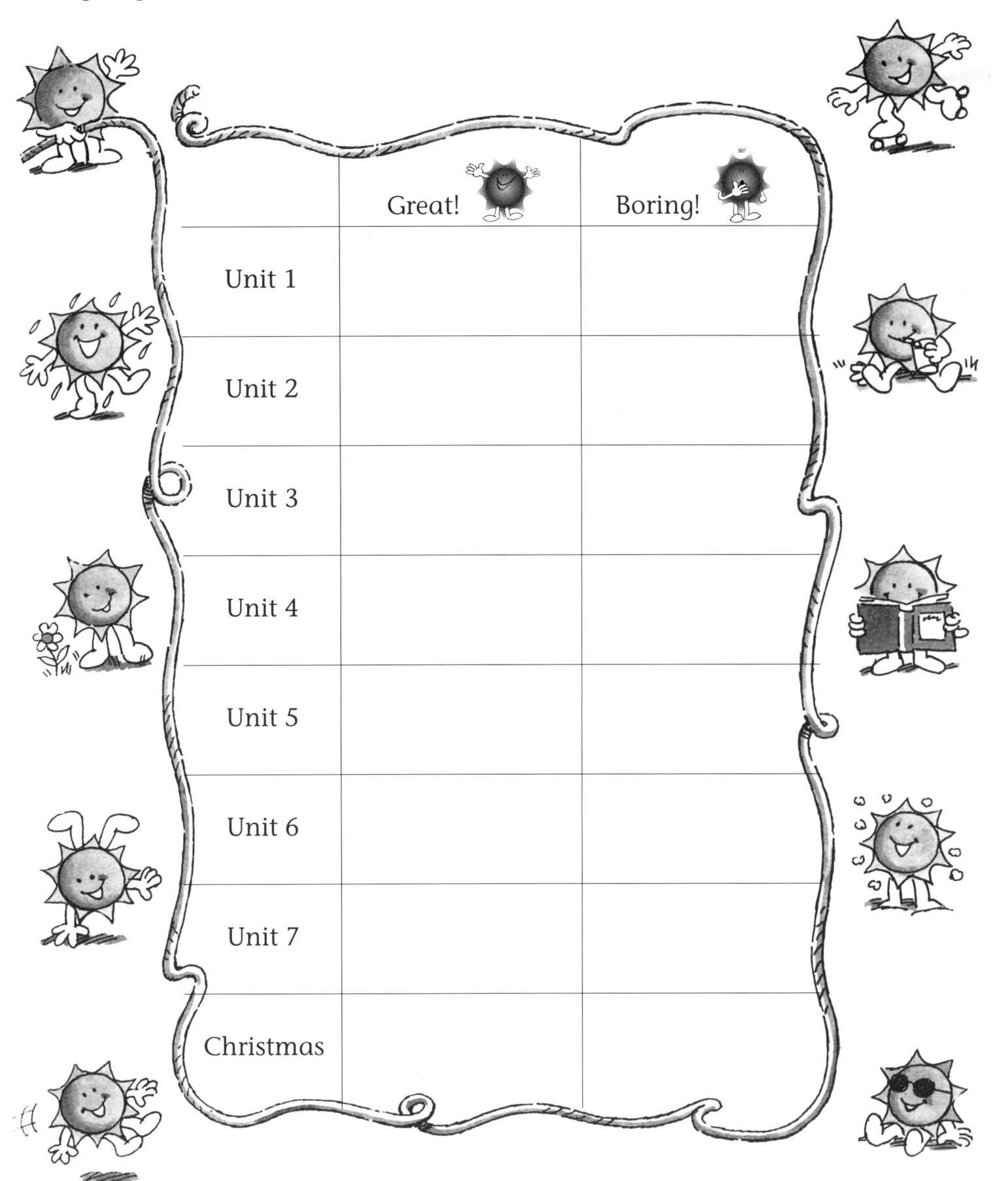

	Great!	Boring!
Unit 1		
Unit 2		
Unit 3		
Unit 4		
Unit 5		
Unit 6		
Unit 7		
Christmas		

Macmillan Heinemann English Language Teaching, Oxford

A division of Macmillan Publishers Limited

Companies and representatives throughout the world

ISBN 0 435 29301X

Based on Say It In English language pack
© Dorling Kindersley Limited & World Book Inc.
Original material used by permission of Dorling Kindersley Limited.

Text, design and illustration © Macmillan Publishers Limited 1998

Heinemann is a registered trademark of Reed Educational & Professional Publishing Limited

First published 1998

All rights reserved; no part of this publication may be reproduced, stored in a retrieval system, transmitted in any form, or by any means, electronic, mechanical, photocopying, recording, or otherwise, without the prior written permission of the publishers.

Designed by The Junction.
Illustrated by Teri Gower, Dewi Morris and David Till

Cover illustrated by Teri Gower and designed by Sue Vaudin

Printed and bound in Spain by Mateu Cromo S.A.

98 99 00 01 10 9 8 7 6 5 4 3 2 1